Oh No, Another Homemade Christmas Present

by
Joshua Crocker

ISBN: 979-8-9879131-5-4 (paperback)

Library of Congress Control Number: 2024925512

Cover design by Joshua Crocker.

Page design by Joshua Crocker.

Paperback print. First edition 2024.

Published by the Paragon Coalition.
Norman, OK
paragoncoalition.com

Dedicated to
Samantha, Eliana,
Caleb, and Jonas

Other Works by Joshua

One Day I'll Know
Snippets of Ink
Songs About Self-Defense
November Storm

Table of Contents

The Going Has Gone

How long till we face the facts
that the past is just another pile of ashes?
They say it's where we're going,
but kid, the going has already gone.
One by one, they sing, each story is written a line at a time.
How many miles between us before we realize
that we're not going anywhere together.
Hey, it's time for me to go. I've got to get up early.

I'm off to some place new. I've got a seat with a view,
and you're not in the spot next to me. We said we'd go together,
but you're off to some place new. A place without me there next to you.

There was an unwritten rule, a promised that went unsaid,
that I would always be there, and you would always do the same.
But here we are, so far away.
Even when I see you, there's a distance between us.

How long till we face the facts
that the past is just another pile of ashes?
They say it's where we're going,
but kid, the going has already gone.
One by one, they sing, each story is written a line at a time.
How many miles between us before we realize
that we're not going anywhere together.
Hey, it's time for me to go. I've got an assignment due.

I'm beginning to believe the things I say.
I watch as you walk off another way,
and I begin to realize some deeper truth.
We said we'd stay forever,
but we're not the same people as yesterday.
People who said they would never go away.

We had something in common,
call it some common dream
or just plain love for one another.
I could always count on you for a talk,
but we're not talking much anymore.
Even when I see you,
there's a distance between us.

How long till we face the facts
that the past is just another pile of ashes?
They say it's where we're going,
but kid, the going has already gone.
One by one, they sing, each story is written a line at a time.
How many miles between us before we realize
that we're not going anywhere together.
Hey, it's time for me to go. I've got plans tonight.

I'm not really looking forward to Christmas this year

< You have one unheard message. >
< First message sent yesterday at 11:23pm. >

Hey, uh, it's getting late out.
I miss when it was still light out when I got home.
So, yeah, I guess it's whatever.
I'm going to be honest,
I'm not really looking forward to Christmas this year.
I mean, I feel like this is a time for celebration and relaxing,
but I feel more indifferent than anything.
I don't have much to celebrate at the moment
and I've been far too anxious lately to relax.
I guess I've just been moody recently.
With the election and everything, then there's this girl...
Nevermind, it's not important.
I can't be the only one who feels this way, right?
I mean, let's be real, this Christmas just feels different.
Money has been tight, and I know I never really cared about
the presents that much, but that's kind of what this entire
holiday is based around. And don't give me the whole
'It's-about-family-and-Jesus' speech.
I'm old enough to know the truth.
It's not just that, this year has just been strange, okay?
Grandma and Grandpa have been in the hospital,
and this season just feels emptier without them around.
Not to mention, I think we're all just getting older.
Christmas has always been marked by
all the fun us kids have together,
but we've all kind of gone our different ways this year.
My time spent with you has gone down,
while my time spent cleaning dishes has gone up.
I don't know what to do now that I'm the one sitting back
watching my siblings and cousins become their own people.

You have all these accomplishments and interests,
and I'm so proud of each one of you,
but I'm just starting to think you all don't need me anymore.
How long is it before we only
see each other a couple times a year?
Christmas will be less about our antics
and more about just catching up with each other.
I don't know, maybe that's not a bad thing, but still.
No matter how old I got, I was always quick to come up
with some game we could play in the backyard together.
What happens when you're too old for my games?
Anyway. Sorry, I've been rambling again.
I'm just not really looking forward to Christmas this year.
Maybe seasonal depression got ahold of me early.
I don't know, I think there's more to it than that.
Do you really think it'll be any better next year?
Once a tree begins to splinter,
you can't put it back together again.
I've been trying to further my own career
and eventually start my own family.
What happens when I have a whole other set
of Christmas gatherings to be at?
I already have to miss out on seeing certain people,
I'm not going to magically find more time.
I guess it's whatever.
Let's be real, this isn't just about Christmas.
I honestly haven't given the holidays much thought at all.
That's the problem, I think.
I've been too preoccupied with my own life
to really look forward to anything else.
I'm sorry for bothering you.
You can delete this message,
I'm not expecting a response back.
Um, Merry Christmas. I love you.
That at least isn't going to change.

< End of message. >
< To delete this message press sev- >
< Message deleted. End of messages. >

12-24-2004

As we sat on that dark teal carpet in the living room,
what was going through your mind?
Did you have any idea of the person I would be?
Could you tell I would be a talented kicker one day,
or aspiring to be a talented writer some other day?
When you looked at me, what did you see?

I was so mesmerized by the pretty lights on the tree,
I didn't even see the gifts with my name underneath.
It would be years before I ever said thank you.
Did I even realize how much you loved me?
You were all I knew, after all.
So, maybe love was all I knew.

What was it like on that day?
We watched Green Bay clinch the North on TV.
Bush was going to be the face of Time Magazine.
Did things seem just as confusing back then?
Or did looking at me make everything seem simple?
Nowadays everything seems so complicated to me.
What would you say to me if you knew
what my life was like today?

As we sat on that plaid couch in the living room,
what was going through your mind?
Were you wondering what kind of person I would be?
Did you know I would make you proud one day,
or could you tell that I might let you down at times?
What was going through your mind
the evening before you would hold me
on Christmas morning for the first time?

WHAT TO GET

You say you don't know what to get them.
Whatever it is, it has to show how much you care.
Something thoughtful, but not cliché.
Something personable, but not overbearing.
Something unique, but not cheaply made.
You want something that says I love you,
even if it takes 8,660 words to say it.
You would even trade in your watch to find such a gift.
No wonder you always feel you're running out of time.
So, you keep racking your brain,
but none of your ideas seem good enough.
That's the problem when you tie your worth
to the way you feel perceived by others.
You want to get them a gift that shows you care,
because you think then they'll surely care about you.

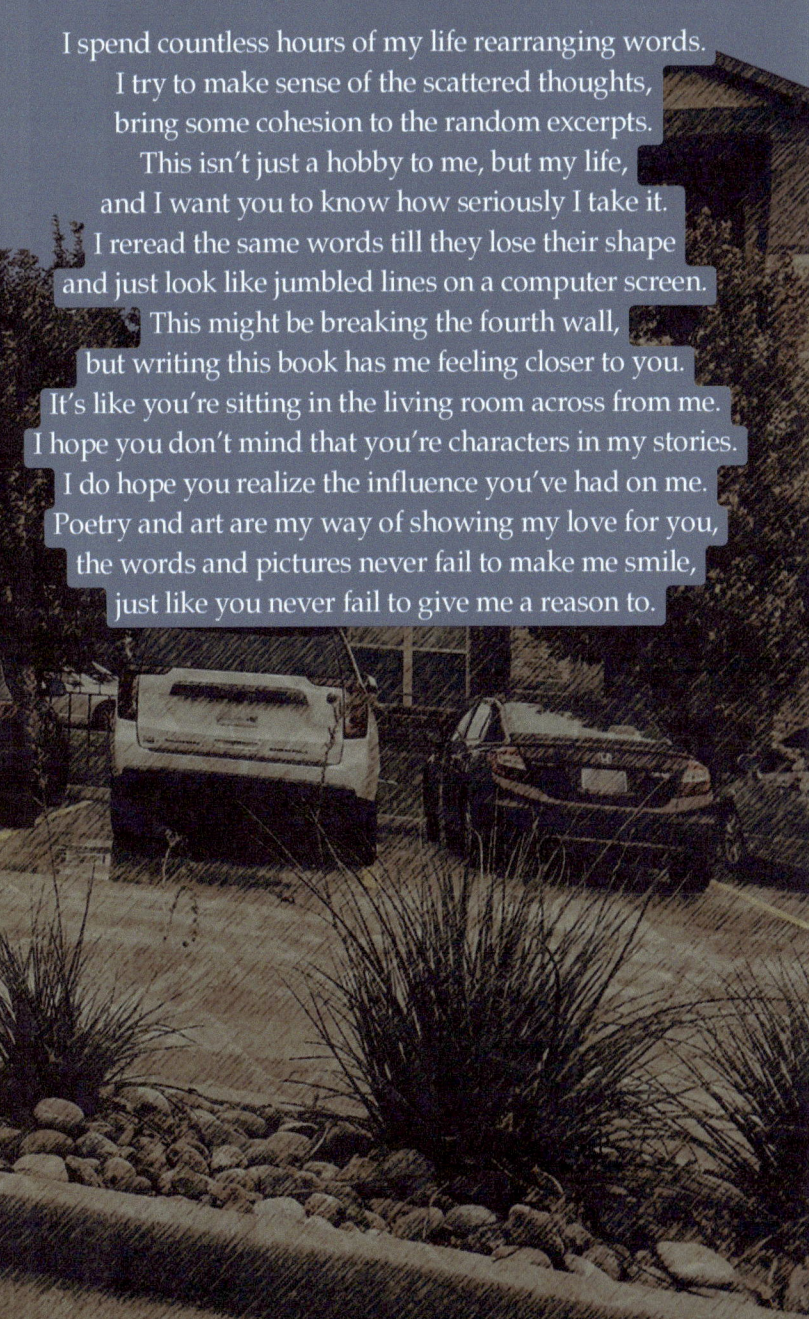

I Really Like Writing

I spend countless hours of my life rearranging words.
I try to make sense of the scattered thoughts,
bring some cohesion to the random excerpts.
This isn't just a hobby to me, but my life,
and I want you to know how seriously I take it.
I reread the same words till they lose their shape
and just look like jumbled lines on a computer screen.
This might be breaking the fourth wall,
but writing this book has me feeling closer to you.
It's like you're sitting in the living room across from me.
I hope you don't mind that you're characters in my stories.
I do hope you realize the influence you've had on me.
Poetry and art are my way of showing my love for you,
the words and pictures never fail to make me smile,
just like you never fail to give me a reason to.

The Murder Files

Dear mercy, it's the day before Christmas
and there's been a murder at the house by the stream.
A classic case of whodunnit?
Let's take a look at the suspects.

The baker speaks with a poor British accent.
They'll bake you a cake or gingerbread cookie.
Holds up a large kitchen knife and says bon appétit.

The toymaker has a scowl on their face.
They've been in this town for half a century.
The door to their workshop is always locked.

The firefighter seems a little full of themself.
They wear a cowboy hat and try to act all tough.
Told me that they love the warmth fire brings.

The editor starts to get a little extra nosy.
They always have a lead or two they're following.
Though the morning paper never gets the story straight.

The actor told me they were a baker at the start.
They say every word with soul-crushing drama.
Can't differentiate between their roles and a lie.

I feel I'm getting close to cracking the case.
Justice shall be given this Christmas.
Just then, a little girl walks up to me with a smile.
She says I can trust her. I ask her what it is she does.
"Don't worry mister. I'm not a murderer."
The girl smiles slyly, and I begin to back away.
"I'm just the minion."
A hand reaches out from the shadow,
taps me on the shoulder twice.
"Goodnight mister."

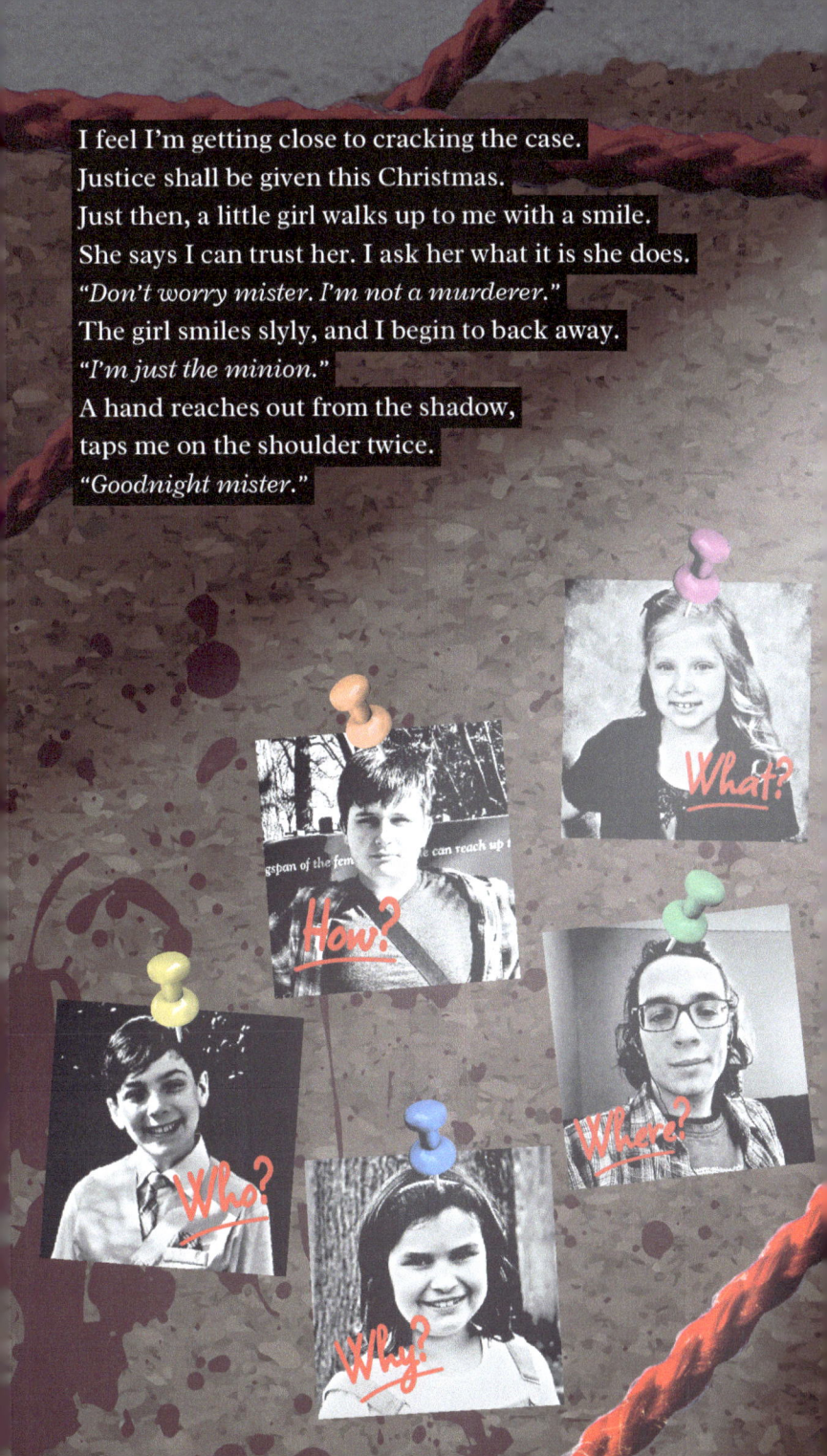

RESISTANCE!

WORKING FOR THE MAN WITH THE LIST.
(HE'S A NO GOOD, OBESE, OLD GEEZER)
CALLOUSES FROM MY FINGERS TO WRIST.
(HE'S A SICK, ROTTEN, REINDEER BEATER)
SWEATING IN HIS WORKSHOP FROM DUSK TO DAWN.
WE'VE HAD ENOUGH!
THIS IS THE END FOR THE MAN WITH THE LIST.
(HE'S GOING TO SLEEP SOUNDLY TONIGHT)
MY BROTHERS, HEAR THE CALL, IT'S TIME TO RESIST!

RULES FROM HIS THRONE WITH FEAR.
ONLY WORKS ONE DAY A YEAR.
HOW DO YOU MAKE IT AROUND THE WORLD IN ONE NIGHT?
YOU GONNA TELL 'EM WHERE YOU MAKE UP THE TIME?
CHECK THAT LIST AGAIN FOR A LIST OF COMMITTED CRIME.
BREAKING DOWN OUR UNION TO PRODUCE HIS GOODS.
SKIPPING THE UNDERPRIVILEGED NEIGHBORHOODS.
THIS CHRISTMAS THERE AIN'T NO EQUALITY!
YOUR NAUGHTY LIST IS A DOG WHISTLE FOR POVERTY.
LET'S PUT AN END TO THIS MERRY MOCKERY.

BURN THE RED COAT! BURN THE RED COAT MAN!
BURN THE RED COAT! BURN IT TILL HE'S DEAD.
WE'LL NEVER BE FREE IF WE DON'T FIGHT FOR OUR RIGHTS.
(HE'S GOING TO SLEEP WITH THE SUGAR PLUMS TONIGHT)

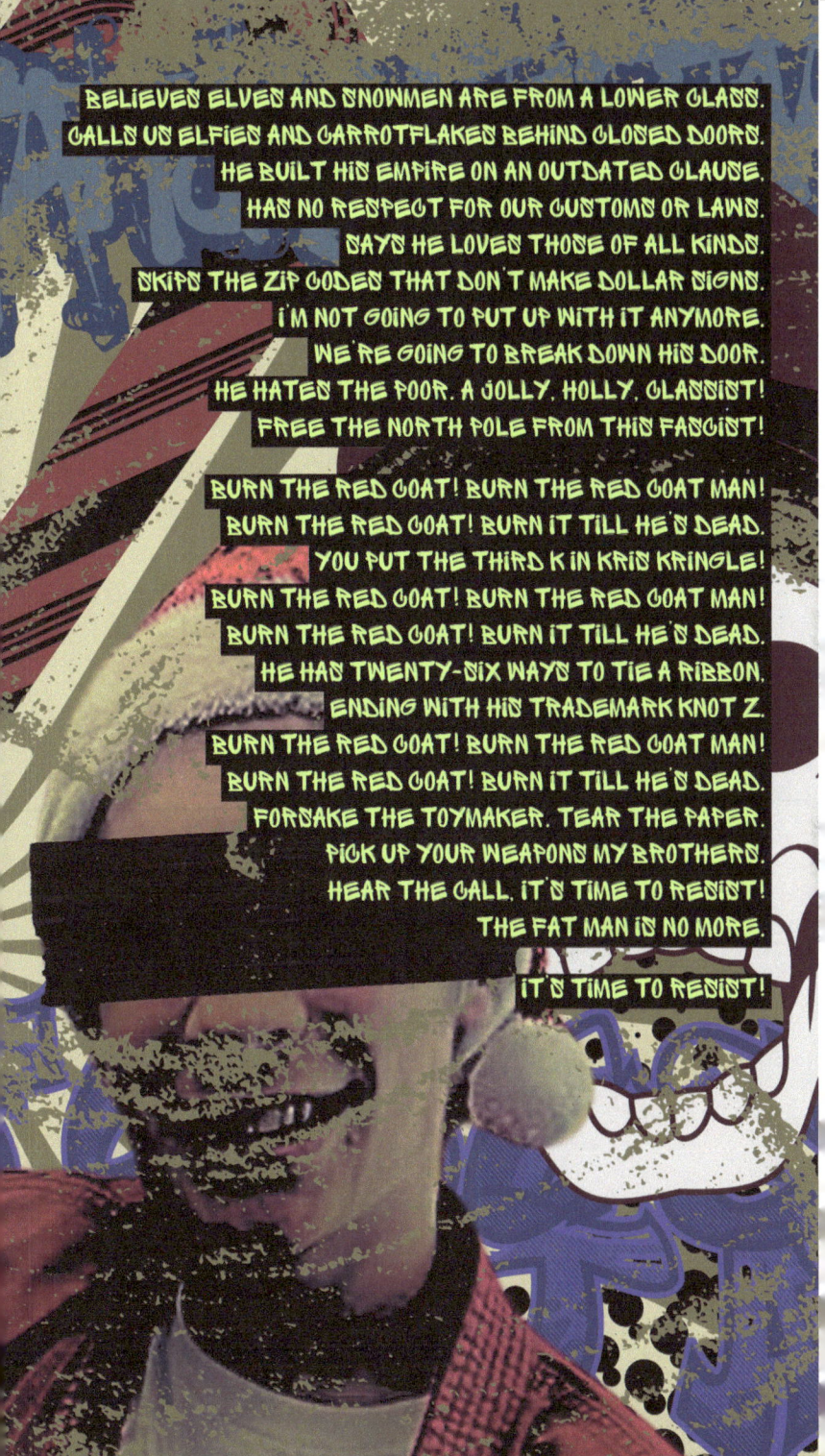

BELIEVES ELVES AND SNOWMEN ARE FROM A LOWER CLASS.
CALLS US ELFIES AND CARROTFLAKES BEHIND CLOSED DOORS.
HE BUILT HIS EMPIRE ON AN OUTDATED CLAUSE.
HAS NO RESPECT FOR OUR CUSTOMS OR LAWS.
SAYS HE LOVES THOSE OF ALL KINDS.
SKIPS THE ZIP CODES THAT DON'T MAKE DOLLAR SIGNS.
I'M NOT GOING TO PUT UP WITH IT ANYMORE.
WE'RE GOING TO BREAK DOWN HIS DOOR.
HE HATES THE POOR. A JOLLY, HOLLY, CLASSIST!
FREE THE NORTH POLE FROM THIS FASCIST!

BURN THE RED COAT! BURN THE RED COAT MAN!
BURN THE RED COAT! BURN IT TILL HE'S DEAD.
YOU PUT THE THIRD K IN KRIS KRINGLE!
BURN THE RED COAT! BURN THE RED COAT MAN!
BURN THE RED COAT! BURN IT TILL HE'S DEAD.
HE HAS TWENTY-SIX WAYS TO TIE A RIBBON.
ENDING WITH HIS TRADEMARK KNOT Z.
BURN THE RED COAT! BURN THE RED COAT MAN!
BURN THE RED COAT! BURN IT TILL HE'S DEAD.
FORSAKE THE TOYMAKER. TEAR THE PAPER.
PICK UP YOUR WEAPONS MY BROTHERS.
HEAR THE CALL. IT'S TIME TO RESIST!
THE FAT MAN IS NO MORE.

IT'S TIME TO RESIST!

Tradition

Never any change, things stay the same.
History repeats itself and repeats itself,
and here we are again.
So much of who we are is built on what we've been told.
So much of these holidays are built on tradition.
It seems we've confused joy with nostalgia.
And I may be guilty too, I tend to be a bit sentimental,
but I don't see the value in something so fundamental.
Tradition just for the sake of it,
repeat the same mistakes time and time again.
We're not going anywhere!
No, we're just living in fear.
Afraid of something different and the things
we don't understand. I see it all around me,
family and friends obsessed with conserving
something I don't really think is worth preserving.
You've romanticized the past,
granted I do this all the time,
but this yesteryear you live in was never great,
in fact, it never even existed.
You just miss a time when things seemed simple.
Back when the stories they told us were in black and white,
and it was as easy being naughty or nice.

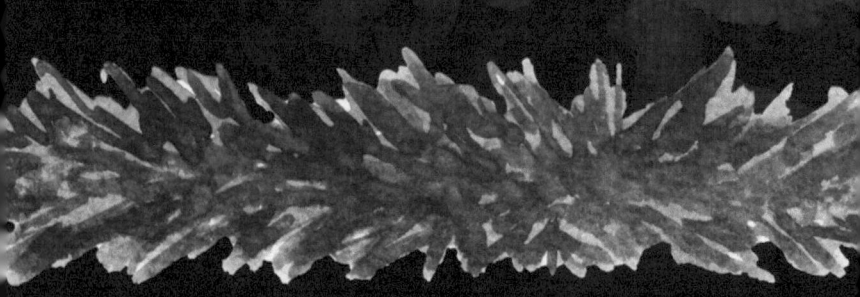

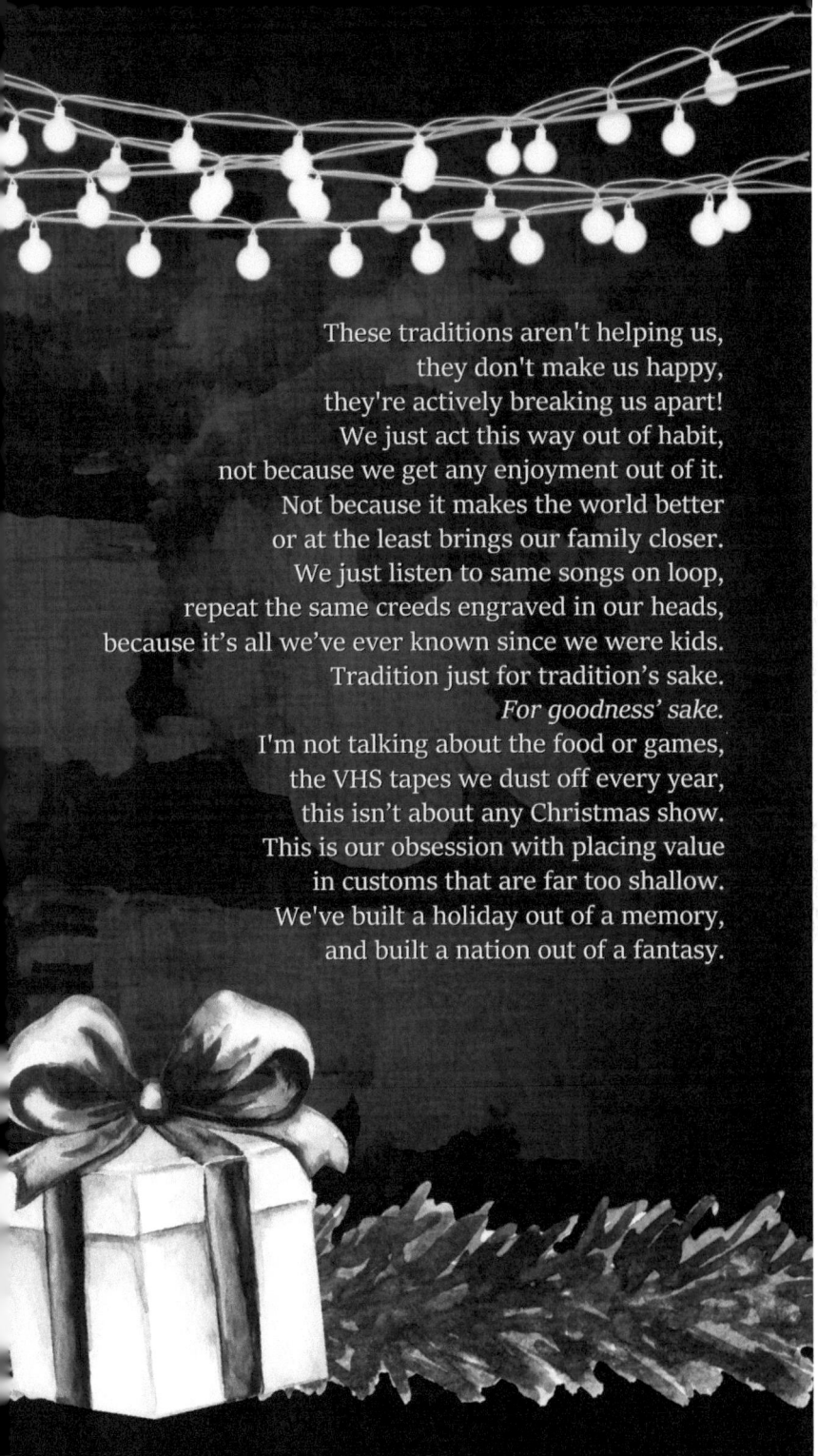

These traditions aren't helping us,
they don't make us happy,
they're actively breaking us apart!
We just act this way out of habit,
not because we get any enjoyment out of it.
Not because it makes the world better
or at the least brings our family closer.
We just listen to same songs on loop,
repeat the same creeds engraved in our heads,
because it's all we've ever known since we were kids.
Tradition just for tradition's sake.
For goodness' sake.
I'm not talking about the food or games,
the VHS tapes we dust off every year,
this isn't about any Christmas show.
This is our obsession with placing value
in customs that are far too shallow.
We've built a holiday out of a memory,
and built a nation out of a fantasy.

Symbols Ringing

So, what do you think? You were born some two thousand years ago, and people still sing songs of joy and praise. We take a whole month of the year just to remember an increasingly mythologized story. Are you honored? Does it make the pain seem worth it? Does this anxious, manic, wasteful holiday make you smile?

We place a star on a tree, claim it will guide us like it did the shepherds. I don't think we give it a second thought. We paint you and your mother in grace, a symbol of what, our overconsumption and greed? I don't see any love for mothers or their sons in this land.

A humble birth turned into a trillion-dollar industry. Gifts of gold to gifts in plastic wrap. Tradition and music that don't make any sense. Now we argue over how to greet each other because it creates more ad revenue for the networks. Are you honored? Does saying, 'Merry Christmas,' make the pain worth it?

My prayers are nothing about you, they're all about me. My struggles and sins, my thoughts and wins. Does this angst-riddled poem mean anything to you, or did I just need a page to fill in my book? I don't know if I've ever honestly cared about you outside of the symbol you supposedly stand for.

So, what do you think? Past the miracles, past the salvation, they say you were a person just like me. You were a kid who I'm sure just wanted to feel warm and loved. I know the feeling. Instead you've become a symbol of whatever we desire, both good and bad. Are you honored? Does this lavish, extravagant pageant of a holiday leave you feeling loved?

For I saw the star rise and come to worship you,
rejoice exceedingly with a great joy,
and on earth may there be peace.

I'm Not an Elf

I'm not an elf, I'm just short.
And sure, I toil away all day writing stories,
and I have created my own board game,
but I promise I'm just your typical guy.

I know I seem cold on the outside,
but that doesn't make me a snowman.
I'm just shy, okay.

I'm not an elf, I just like the color green.
And sure, I'm another victim of Santa's
capitalistic present giving machine,
but I assure you I'm just your average Joe.

I know people only pretend to like me,
but that doesn't make me a fruitcake.
I'm just short, okay.

I'm not an elf, I just have long hair.
And sure, I like to climb up on shelves,
and I have a mischievous smile,
but I can confidently say I'm normal. Mostly.

I'm not an elf.
I don't know why people keep asking.
I'm just short.

Hollow Words

I walk in the forest.
The wind calls, I feel it brush against my hips.
The trees are dead and hollow,
waiting for the day they'll bloom.
Sometimes I relate to them.

I talk with my family.
I don't call much, but we see each other often.
The words we say are hollow,
but I don't know whether it's you or me.
I guess in a way it might be both.

The concept of unconditional love entertains me.
Is love strong enough to keep us together
no matter what life has in store?
Nowadays everything has a price tag.
What is my name worth to you?

We only share words at face value.
If there is nothing deeper,
what is going to root us together?
When the wind comes, the hollow tree will break,
and likewise our love is at stake.

I wrote you a Christmas card,
the signature on it is a little shaky.
I told you I hate the way it looks,
you said I shouldn't worry about it.
I don't think you quite get it.

Where are you going to draw the line?
What would it take for me
to not be invited to Christmas dinner?
Nothing you say. You'll love me forever and ever.
I don't know, those words sound hollow to me.

I've been told not to bother with hypotheticals,
but I've been told a lot of things,
and I've told my share of lies.
I try not to be melodramatic,
but wintertime brings the worst out of me.

I walk in the forest.
The wind calls, pushing my hair against my face.
I don't want to feel hollow anymore,
but that's easier said than done.
Maybe you'll understand one day.

I talk with my family.
I don't call much, I've never felt the need to.
The air around us sings a foreboding song,
yet I have faith that you'll always be here.
I promise you it isn't a hollow faith.

Promise me your words aren't hollow either.

Do You Know Where We Are?

Another year together, growing further apart.
You recognize this place? Because I do.
This is the same spot we were in last time.
We started fighting, trying not to turn it to screaming.
We never said I love you. Do we ever anymore?
I don't want to leave, I don't want you to leave me,
but I think it's time for us to go.

Do you know where we are?
We stop by the Pretzel Eleven and Old Bookshop.
We share what we know. We smile and joke,
trying to avoid the sad reality of this place.

We would walk together. We could talk together.
The schemes, the games, they were ours.
I went through a bin of old photos.
What happened to those kids?
You used to be in the room near mine.
You were never more than a call away.
I look around now, you're all gone.

Do you think we'll ever be friends again

Do you know who we are?
My friend, have you noticed the sadness in my eyes?
Life has gotten more complicated than we thought.
And I can tell you feel the same way.

Things seemed a little simpler around you.
We were writing a story on the same line,
and we fell in love with the words each time.
Did we take for granted what we had?
We're trying to forget that things tend to change.
We ignore the rips in an already torn tapestry.
I sit by the fire alone now, not all of us here.

Do you know how we are?
This probably means more than we want to admit.
Did they tell us growing up means moving on?
If so, I'm not ready to say goodbye.

Another year together, growing further apart.
You recognize this place? Because I do.
This is the same spot we were in last time.
We started fighting, trying not to turn it to screaming.
We never said I love you. Do we ever anymore?
I don't want to leave, I don't want you to leave me,
but I think it's time for us to go.

Do you know where we are?
Because it's not the same place we used to be.
Why does growing up have to mean moving on?
I'm not ready to say goodbye.

Maybe. But right now,
I think we both need to move on.

THE THANKSGIVING SONG

I've been saying for a couple weeks now
I was going to write a Thanksgiving song.
It would be a good exercise in gratitude.
Unfortunately, I don't have the best attitude.
What is there to be thankful for?
Right now I can't think of much.
Would you tell me, please?
Pretty please, I'll even add a cherry.

I guess I should use the first verse to clarify.
Get the standard platitude of gratitude out of the way.
I'll say thanks for my home and a roof above,
clothes and shoes, a good job that pays the bills.
I'm grateful for all this food, though I don't eat much.
I'm thankful for my family, though I don't know if
they'll be so thrilled with the way I vilify them.
I'm grateful for my friends, though it's a one-way street.
There you go; you happy now? I said thanks.
Can we stop holding hands now? This is getting weird.

What are you thankful for? Who are you singing to?
I don't know. Well maybe I do, but I won't say.
What are you grateful for? Who are you clinging to?
I won't tell you. Well maybe I will, but not right now.
I don't want to regret saying thanks,
if it turns out what I had was never mine.
If I am so blessed, why am I this stressed?

The second verse isn't going to go any better.
I'll tell you the magnitude of my attitude isn't great.
The takeaway from this year was that people aren't good
and my twenties are going to be weird.
I'll be grateful when my nerves aren't on fire.
I'll be thankful when I no longer have to plan a
different disguise for every other day of the week.
I'll be grateful when I write a story that comes true.
There we go; now no one's happy. I won't say thanks.
Can we just start eating now? Sorry to ruin the mood.

On to the bridge, where I ramble on about that time
when I wrote a few generic thank you cards.
Thank you for, blah-blah, and so on.
It was the same message a couple dozen times.
I promise I give thanks every day, but there's nothing
I hate more than when all my prayers sound the same.
I want my words to sound real.
If I could, I would write a letter to everyone I love,
go in depth about how much you mean to me.
But I won't. Because, well, what if you don't read it?
What does that say about me?
I don't know if I want to know.

What are you thankful for? Who are you singing to?
I don't know. Well maybe I do, but I won't say.
What are you grateful for? Who are you clinging to?
I won't tell you. Well maybe I will, but not right now.
I don't want to regret saying thanks,
if it turns out what I had was never mine.
If I am so blessed, why am I this stressed?

I really am trying to remember to give thanks.
I want to be the kind of person you are to me.
So, when you give grace, I hope you think of me.

End of the Year

My friend, I don't want this year to end.
I'm not ready to start back at January.
Let's just stay here together.
We don't have to turn the page yet.
Please, I don't want this year to end.

The thought of next year scares me.
I've made it so far; I don't want to start over.
And I know that sounds ridiculous,
time doesn't work like that.
I feel like this is my last chance though,
my last chance to do something great this year.
Because what exactly have I accomplished so far?
The short-sighted answer is not much.
Maybe that's why I've been spending countless hours
writing this book, just so I can wrap it up in a nice bow.

Am I a better person than I was last year?
How would I even know?
I've felt calmer and less stressed,
but the feeling doesn't always last.
I keep procrastinating on honest conversation.
There are still so many people I need to say
Merry Christmas to before the days arrives.
I have to tell them thank you.
I have to tell them I love them.
I want them to know before the year is over.

My friend, I don't want this year to end.
Please just stay here with me,
we don't have to say goodnight if we never go to sleep.
I'm afraid I've missed out on too much time,
I fear next year won't be as great.
So, please stay. I don't want this to end.

Carols and Hymns

I love to sing, though I question if I'm any good.
I'm tone deaf, though I know how to read the room.

You've heard them before,
and you know you'll hear them again.

I love the carols we sing,
I love the hymns we read.

Sometimes I try so hard to hit the right notes,
I forget to read the words I'm saying.

I sing with more emotion than talent,
and I love every beat and every breath.

I believe that music has influenced me more
than most speeches or books ever could.

I repeat song lyrics in my head all the time,
be they from the hymnal, radio, or my journal.

Never felt more at ease then when I sing,
surrounded by the people I love.

I love to sing, I love to hear your voice next to mine.
Let's sing carols of cheer, let's sing hymns together.

FROG

Would you love me if I was a frog?
Kiss me on my froggy cheek.
Would you love me if I was a thief on the run?
Help me hide away from the police.
Would you love me if I let you down?
I'm not trying to, but I fear I might.

Don't say I don't love you,
I most definitely do.
I hope the feeling goes both ways,
just say you love me too.

Would you love me if I grew a third eyeball?
Say I have really pretty tri-eyes.
Would you love me if I left town for a while?
Call me every week just to check in on life.
Would you love me if I say something you don't like?
Just know I was never trying to hurt you.

Don't say I don't love you,
I most definitely do.
I hope the feeling goes both ways,
just say you love me too.

Would you love me if I was a piece of cheese?
Tell me I look very Gouda today.
Would you love me if I started a revolution?
Walk the street arm in arm with me.
Would you love me if I'm honest with you?
Because honestly, that's where I need your love most

Crying Used to Be Easy

When I was little it wasn't hard to find
a reason to cry your eyes out.
Scraped my knee, my sister said something mean,
or maybe I was simply hungry.
It used to be easy to be sad.
Anymore, sad thoughts are so much more.
Inside every single one of these tears
is a quiet reflection of my worst fears.
Lack of control, loss of love, failure of self.
I don't mean to get emotional,
the more I feel, the more there is at stake.

I Maed This Four You

The year was 1987, back when his little girl was still little. He asked his boss if he could leave early. His boss replied with a stern maybe. Five o'clock rolled around, the sun had already begun to set. He hurried to his car and pulled out onto the streets of Omaha.

He arrived at the bank, paycheck in hand. The lights were already dim inside, both doors locked. He glanced at the watch on his wrist, but it didn't matter, the thing had been broken for weeks. With a sigh, he rummaged through the pockets of his wallet. All he found was a folded ten and a couple of singles. He told himself that would have to be enough.

Shoulder to shoulder, people filled the department store. With a piece of construction paper in his hand, he squeezed his way to the back of the store. The list he held had one and only one thing written on it. Scribbled in green crayon, it said, Astragold Doll.

He searched the nearly empty shelves for the toy. On the top shelf, behind a knocked over Barbie playset, there was still one doll left. Under his breath he prayed a quick thank you before grabbing the toy from its spot.

The line to the register was at least ten minutes long. He stood there, patiently tapping his foot. In front of him was a grandmother with her cart full of racecars and pink dresses. Behind him a mother scolded her screaming child. After what seemed like an eternity of counting bills, the old lady in front of him went on her merry way. He placed the doll down in front of the cashier and fished for his wallet, a terrible realization occurring to him. That very wallet was currently sitting on the dashboard of his car.

"Excuse me, sir. Any day now," the woman behind him said.

He turned to the cashier, "I forgot my wallet in my car. Can you hold my item for me?"

"I'm sorry sir, but it's against company policy to hold items during holiday shopping," the cashier responded.

He sat the doll down; with a desperate plea he told it not to move. He sprinted into the parking lot, nearly getting ran over by a red Corvette. Taking his wallet from its spot, he was in such a rush he forgot to lock his car again. Back inside, he returned to where he left the doll, only to find an empty spot.

He drove home in the dark, not even sure how late it was. Hopefully his dinner hadn't gotten cold. Just north of the railroad tracks was a little house surrounded by dead grass. Stepping out of his car, he was met by a cold breeze blowing in from the Missouri River. He fidgeted with the broken door handle, the one he had promised to fix when he had the cash. Inside he found his daughter coloring at the kitchen table. He was too ashamed to make eye contact with her, missing her little wave hello.

The next morning he sat in the cramped living room, his daughter smiling in front of him. His wife handed him a plate of cornbread casserole. As they ate their food, his little girl kept talking about how excited she was to open the gift waiting for her under the tree. A sense of guilt would fill him as he watched her rip open the wrapping paper, the present she asked for not present at all.

Torn paper lay on the carpet next to his daughter. "He's so cute!" she cried, holding up a little stuffed brontosaurus. The toy let out a static-y snore. "He even makes noise! This is the most awesomest present ever," she said with a huge grin.

The girl at once paused, as if she had just realized something important. "Hold on a second." She sat the toy down slowly and ran out of the room. He just sat there, contemplating what kind of father he was. He couldn't even let the simplest of his daughter's wishes come true.

His little girl returned with a crudely wrapped present of her own. She handed it to her dad. "This is for you."

He carefully removed the wrapping paper, revealing a collection of drawings of all her favorite memories with her dad. At the top of the page, I Maed This Four You, was written in red crayon. His eyes began tearing up as he looked at all the details she had included in her drawings. There wasn't a picture where the little stick figures weren't smiling ear to ear. He turned the page over, written in big letters across the back, it said, I Love You Daddy.

"I wanted to get you a new watch, but mommy said we couldn't afford it right now, so I made this for you instead," the girl told her dad. "I hope you like it."

"I love it!" he said, wiping a tear from his cheek. He pulled his daughter in close for a hug. "And I love you so much."

The year was 2021, his little girl not so little anymore. Out in the suburbs of Omaha, he sat in his living room, plenty of room for the entire family. He smiled, after a year of not being able to see each other, his daughter had returned home. She had a family her own now, her kids running around, more than excited to open the pile of gifts under the tree.

He had just finished helping his wife prepare breakfast, as he sat down in his recliner to watch his grandkids tear into their presents. They eventually got to a gift labeled for him. His daughter handed it to him.

"I got this for you," she said with a smile. He opened it. A brand-new watch was inside. "I remember you saying how hard it was for you to tell time on your watch, so I got you one with bigger numbers on it."

In jest, he adjusted his glasses and squinted. "It's perfect. Thank you," he said.

Later that night, the kids were playing with their new toys. The TV was showing Christmas specials on repeat. He walked into the kitchen to find his daughter eating a piece of pie. "I'm so glad you all are able to be here again."

"So am I," she said. "It's been another great Christmas."

He pulled his little girl in close. "I love you," he said.

"I love you too, dad."

Fifteen Years

If you wouldn't mind,
could you check my math for me.
I took us and added fifteen years,
and the result was we're all doing pretty awesome.
The only way I see it,
another decade or two with you
will be another decade or two well spent.
I don't really care we're we live,
be it Oklahoma or New York, Chicago or wherever else,
we'll still be friends and you'll still be family.

No natural disaster or loss will stop me
from coming back around to see you.
There's not a spot on earth that will keep me
from thinking about how much I love you.

If you wouldn't mind,
could you check my math for me.
I took us and added fifteen years,
and the result was we all still love each other.
The only way I see it,
every memory or moment with you
is another memory or moment worth keeping.
I'm not too concerned with the details,
be they dramatic or cartoonish, boring or whatever else,
we'll still be writing a story worth telling.

No Gift Receipt

Who are you going to bring home for Christmas?
It's been another year, what do you have to show for it?
I've been carefully setting aside money
so I can pay for gifts and romantic dates.
The money just sits there though,
haven't really had the need to use it.
I'm not even sure what to get my family,
they say they'll be happy with whatever,
but will have to fake a smile when I hand them this book.
The white elephant gifts were given last week,
sorry, I had to wait for delivery.
I don't mean to disappoint,
maybe that's why I didn't bring a girl with me.
The only places to find a date are church or the bar,
and I'll deal with judgement either way.
Don't look at me weird if we hold hands to pray,
and what does it say about me if she's a little gay.
I'll share all the photos from the year,
but what stories am I keeping to myself?
There's something missing in that slideshow.
What words did I leave between the lines?
This book is based on true stories
but should be categorized as fiction.
Because I've been dreaming about a Christmas
where I'll exchange gifts with the girl I like,
we'll all get along like when I was a kid,
you'll all say I love you, and I'll say it back.
But I won't be bringing anyone home this year.
Merry Christmas, let's hope it's a happy one.

P.S. Sorry there's no gift receipt for this book.

Thank You Note

Endings used to scare me.
I would always put off watching
the final episode of my favorite TV series.
I saved every stat and rough draft
from every project I ever worked on.
I believed the best things in life would last forever.
What does that have to do with you?
Well, lately, I've been trying
to find the beauty in uncertainty.
I'm realizing not all art is permanent.
The words I write today may not
be the words I write tomorrow.
But that doesn't make them any less impactful.
I want to say thank you.
Thank you for being here.
To everyone I love, we may not be perfect,
but I've been learning to love my imperfections.
I want to tell you how thankful I am.
I'm just simply happy when I'm around you.
Why should I be afraid of the future when
the present I have with you is so great?
I want you to know how grateful I am.
Every moment with you is worth being here for,
and even if the moments dry up some day,
I want to say thank you while you're still here.
So, thank you.
Thank you for being a part of my life.

Paper Telephone

Bud, how did we get here?
Y'know I love you, but I fear,
we haven't been very clear with each other.
This one might be on me,
I never claimed to be great at communication;
my form of art is spoken word,
but I haven't quite figured out the spoken part.

I still don't understand
how a turkey dinner turned into a circus.
I still don't understand
why we choose to act like this on purpose.
Are these games we're playing with each other
really the only way we know how to get along?
We say endlessly we love one another,
yet pass on nothing but scribbles and crude lines.

For once can't we just be honest?
There's no need to be clever or cryptic,
I want the words I tell you to just be the words you hear,
not another present turned into a ticking time bomb.
I'm not saying I'm innocent here,
but it takes at least two to communicate.
And I'm tired of it seeming like no one
knows the rules to this game we're playing.

Can we try this one more time tonight?
Maybe we can finally get it right this time.
If my hands begin shaking, I'm sorry,
I tend to get nervous from time to time,
but when I pass you my hastily drawn heart,
I hope you know it means I love you.

MAKING IT UP
AS WE GO

I THOUGHT WE HAD A PLAN WE WERE STICKING TO.
YOU SAID YOU WERE JUST FOLLOWING ME,
BUT I SAID I WOULD LISTEN TO YOU ON THIS ONE.
DON'T TELL ME WE'RE JUST GOING IN BLIND,
I THOUGHT YOU KNEW MORE THAN ME.

LADIES AND GENTS, HOLD YOUR APPLAUSE.
IT'S TIME FOR YOUR MAIN EVENT.
BABY, HERE WE GO!
THEY THINK WE'VE GOT THIS FIGURED OUT,
BUT WE'RE JUST MAKING IT UP AS WE GO.
ONE STEP AT A TIME, THEY SAY,
WE'LL FIGURE IT OUT EVENTUALLY.
NO ONE SAID LIFE WOULD BE PARTICULARLY EASY,
I DON'T KNOW WHY I THOUGHT IT WOULD BE,
BUT IF WE QUIT NOW, WE'LL NEVER GET TO THE FUN PART.

YOU'VE GOT A BOY ON YOUR MIND
AND I'VE GOT MY EYES ON THAT GIRL.
YOU'RE TRYING TO SOLVE EQUATIONS
WHILE I'M TRYING TO PAY MY BILLS.
WE'VE ALL GOT A LESSON OR TWO TO LEARN,
BUT WE'LL LEARN MORE AFTER WE BEGIN.
WHAT ARE WE WAITING FOR KID? LET'S GO!

FLIP A COIN AT THE FORK IN THE ROAD.
FREESTYLE WHEN THE BEAT GOES MISSING.
WE MAY NOT BE SURE OF EVERYTHING,
BUT I'M SURE WE'LL FIGURE IT OUT TOGETHER.

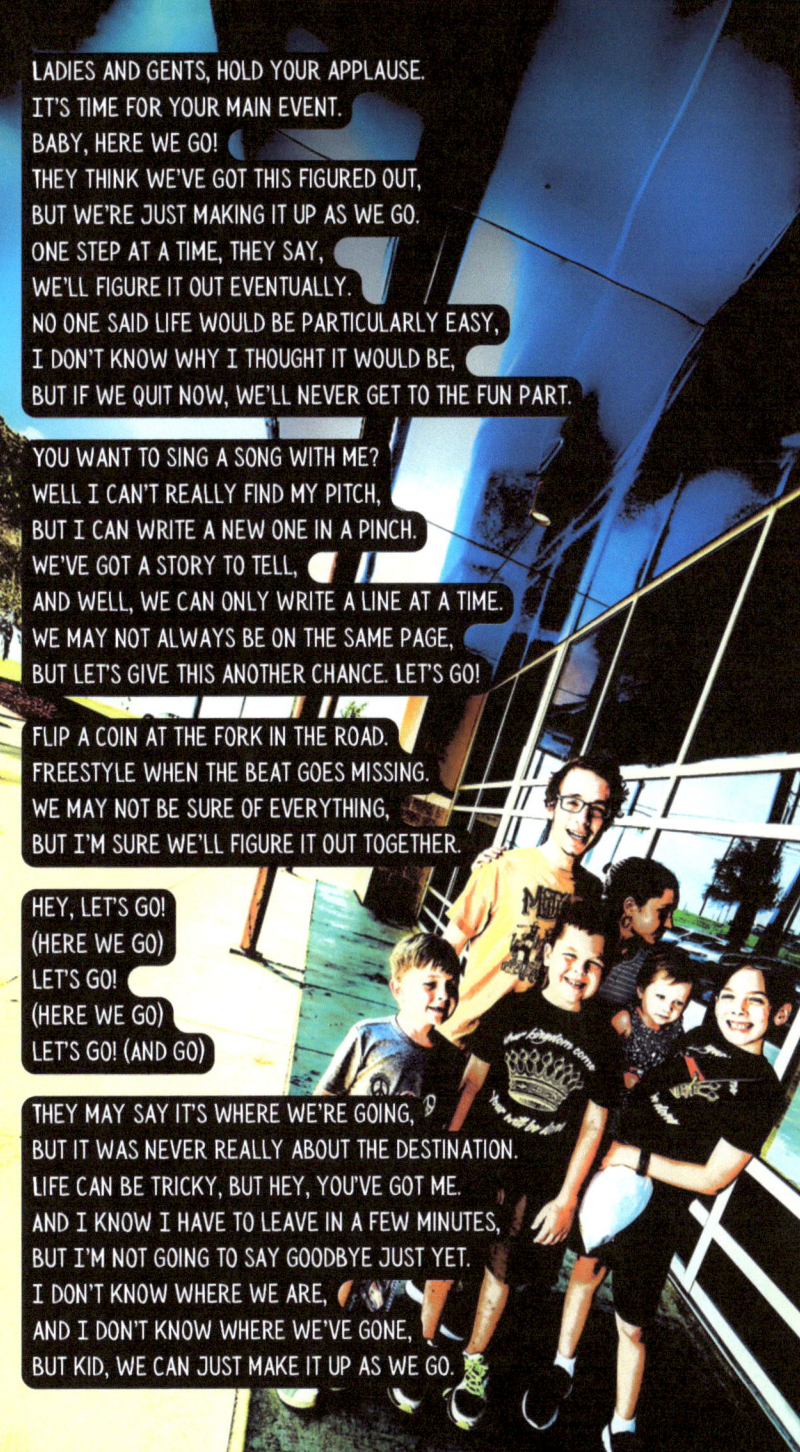

LADIES AND GENTS, HOLD YOUR APPLAUSE.
IT'S TIME FOR YOUR MAIN EVENT.
BABY, HERE WE GO!
THEY THINK WE'VE GOT THIS FIGURED OUT,
BUT WE'RE JUST MAKING IT UP AS WE GO.
ONE STEP AT A TIME, THEY SAY,
WE'LL FIGURE IT OUT EVENTUALLY.
NO ONE SAID LIFE WOULD BE PARTICULARLY EASY,
I DON'T KNOW WHY I THOUGHT IT WOULD BE,
BUT IF WE QUIT NOW, WE'LL NEVER GET TO THE FUN PART.

YOU WANT TO SING A SONG WITH ME?
WELL I CAN'T REALLY FIND MY PITCH,
BUT I CAN WRITE A NEW ONE IN A PINCH.
WE'VE GOT A STORY TO TELL,
AND WELL, WE CAN ONLY WRITE A LINE AT A TIME.
WE MAY NOT ALWAYS BE ON THE SAME PAGE,
BUT LET'S GIVE THIS ANOTHER CHANCE. LET'S GO!

FLIP A COIN AT THE FORK IN THE ROAD.
FREESTYLE WHEN THE BEAT GOES MISSING.
WE MAY NOT BE SURE OF EVERYTHING,
BUT I'M SURE WE'LL FIGURE IT OUT TOGETHER.

HEY, LET'S GO!
(HERE WE GO)
LET'S GO!
(HERE WE GO)
LET'S GO! (AND GO)

THEY MAY SAY IT'S WHERE WE'RE GOING,
BUT IT WAS NEVER REALLY ABOUT THE DESTINATION.
LIFE CAN BE TRICKY, BUT HEY, YOU'VE GOT ME.
AND I KNOW I HAVE TO LEAVE IN A FEW MINUTES,
BUT I'M NOT GOING TO SAY GOODBYE JUST YET.
I DON'T KNOW WHERE WE ARE,
AND I DON'T KNOW WHERE WE'VE GONE,
BUT KID, WE CAN JUST MAKE IT UP AS WE GO.

coffee and Lights

Story #4: A Hypothetical

*"Hey, would you want to grab coffee and go see
the Christmas lights? It's just that, I think you're
really cool and kinda cute, and well..."*
No, that sounds stupid. Just forget about it already.
You know it'll never happen.

Story #2: A Jacket Around My Waist

Don't walk backwards they tell me,
a lesson I learned a few seconds too late.
Now there's a jacket around my waist.
I walk faster than most,
so rather than slow down, I walk alone.

Story #3: A 42-19 Victory

My cousin texted me while I ate lunch.
"Hey! Do you have any plans tonight?"
Well, I was going to watch the game.
You see, it's a rematch from last year's cha–
*"Do you want to come with me and my family
to see the lights this evening?"*
I don't know. I guess I could drive out a little early.
The game should be done around six after all.
"No worries if you're busy, but I just thought I'd ask!"
I bet I can find a coffee shop. Watch from there. Hmm.
It would give me a chance to work on the script as well.
I'll do it. I let my cousin know I'll be there.
She sends back a smiley face emoji.
"I think it'll be a great night!"

Story #1: A Faded Memory

I remember it being dark out,
but the lights shined bright that night.
My closest friend at the time was with me.
I've known her for the past three and half years,
and I can already tell we'll be friends forever.
Even when she goes to college and I stay close to home,
we'll still see each other at Christmas time.

Story #3: A 42-19 Victory

I sat in a coffee shop in a town I wasn't from.
The game was playing on my phone,
and my latest screenplay was on my laptop screen.
I was writing the lines that we would say together.
"We had a table in the back of the café."
You and I would share over coffee again,
"Sorry, you go," I said. *"No, you go ahead."*
The story said we wouldn't get along in the future,
but I had driven an hour from home
just so I could hang out with you tonight.

Story #1: A Faded Memory

I remember it being cold out,
but you still stood close.
My parents walked with me
as we saw the lights sparkling.
They held me up to get a better view.
We were with family and friends,
and while the memory may be gone, they're not.

Story #2: A Jacket Around My Waist

Don't walk backwards they tell me,
a lesson I learned a few seconds too late.
The worst thing you can hurt is your pride.
I often make a fool of myself,
I worry that's all people see, a complete weirdo.

Story #4: A Hypothetical

I could hold your left hand with my right,
and still have a hand free for my coffee.
That might be a bit brash for me,
I'm nervous just thinking about it,
but maybe we could at least go as friends.
*"It's just that, I like spending time with you,
and I always feel warm inside when you're around..."*
No, you can't say that. Just be casual about it.
"So, I was thinking, it's Christmas time and all..."

Story #1: A Faded Memory

I remember the terror in my eyes,
if there's one thing I know,
it's that I can be a fearful person.
I get startled by my own shadow.
We came across a bridge and I froze.
The chilly water underneath looked like a tomb.
My heart fret with every step.
Back then I was probably little enough to fall
through the cracks in the wooden planks.
Or at least that's what I thought.
All those pretty lights left my mind
as I concentrated on my every step.

Story #2: A Jacket Around My Waist

Don't walk backwards they tell me,
a lesson I learned a few seconds too late.
Now there's a rip in my clothes.
I could have hurt myself,
if only I had slowed down, I would be fine.

Story #3: A 42-19 Victory

My coffee had begun to run low,
and the sun had begun to go below.
I was smiling as my team scored again.
Six touchdowns scored, never was even close.
I've been told I can get a little stressed out at times,
like how I had been writing non-stop for weeks
just so I could finish our Christmas story.
But as I walked out to my car
I didn't have a worry in the world.
"I'll be there soon."
I often get anxious about my favorite things.
Like a bridge covered in Christmas lights
or a night out with friends.
But as I drove across town
I was just excited to hang out with my cousin.
"Great! Look forward to seeing you!"

Story #4: A Hypothetical

It's hard not to be a bit of a romantic in December.
There are all these couples walking together,
and you look so pretty in that sweater.
But if there's one thing I know,
it's that I can be an anxious person.
I get startled by my own thoughts.
*"Sorry if I seem I kinda nervous right now, it's just
that, you always have this way of making me smile..."*
We're surrounded by all these pretty Christmas lights,
but my eyes have been following you all night.
Seeing you here, smiling.
I don't know why I was ever so worried.

Story #1: A Faded Memory

I remember being so afraid,
the cold, dark night sky all I could see.
And when all I wanted to do was hide away,
you stood right by me. You held my hand tightly,
reassured me you wouldn't let me go anywhere.
When we got to the other side,
I saw the lights shine bright again.
You pulled me in close for a photo,
and now no matter how fuzzy my memory gets,
I can still remember you being there for me.

Story #2: A Jacket Around My Waist

Don't walk backwards they tell me,
a lesson I learned a few seconds too late.
Now they won't let me forget the story.
I don't mind that much,
the best part of the story, you were there.

Story #3: A 42-19 Victory

I was proudly wearing a cap with my team's logo,
still taking in the win I had marked
on my calendar all year.
You and I walked around the park,
exploring all the Christmas cheer to be had.
We shared a few inside jokes, made some new ones,
and plotted our own homecoming.
I made sure to pull you in close for a photo,
that way no matter how fuzzy your memory gets,
you can still remember me being there for you.
"Thank you for joining me tonight!"
"I had a great time, and I am so happy you came."
It really was a fun night.
All because I got coffee and saw the lights.
I'm glad you asked me to join you.
"Have a good night!"
And I sure am glad I agreed to go.

Story #1: A Faded Memory

I remember it being dark out,
but the lights shined bright that night.
My closest friend at the time, my sister,
enjoyed a cup of hot cocoa with me,
as we got to see the lights shine together.
We were with family and friends,
and no matter how scared I got,
I remember that they've always been there for me.

Story #4: A Hypothetical

Don't walk backwards they always told me.
A lesson I'm not sure I ever learned.
I've always been one to walk fast.
But you tell me to walk slower, and I do,
because then I get to walk next to you.
"Joshua! You made it!"
I don't know why I was ever so worried.
You always do make me smile.
For fifteen years I've been going out to see the lights.
My family and friends taught me
that no matter how nervous I get,
there have always been people there for me.
I want to be there for all of you.
All I want for Christmas is to make you smile.
Y'know, I've learned something from my cousin.
It never hurts to ask some if they want to
join you for coffee and lights.